Refreshment for the Caregiver's Spirit

LORETTA WOODWARD VENEY

ISBN 979-8-9886783-4-2 Paperback
ISBN 979-8-9886783-6-6 Amazon Paperback
ISBN 979-8-9886783-5-9 eBook
ISBN 979-8-9886783-7-3 Amazon eBook

Published July 2023

Dedication

I dedicate this book to Timothy MacBeth Veney, my biggest cheerleader, best friend of 36 years, soulmate and husband of almost 31 years. This book wouldn't be possible without the amazing photos he took on our many travels and adventures. Tim loved life and lived it to the fullest each and every day. He had a magnetic smile and captivating laugh and impacted the lives of everyone around him. Tim made you feel special even if you only met him once, and he made my Mom feel special on each and every visit, even after she no longer remembered who we were.

When I became an author as part of my fight against Alzheimer's disease, Tim was with me every step of the way. He packed and mailed books all around the country, and entertained folks standing in line at my book signings. Tim knew I was working on this book to lift the spirits of Caregivers, and he was thrilled that some of his favorite photos would become part of the book. I'm devastated that he died after a very short illness on July 17, 2016, but he lives on in the lives of all of us who knew and loved him. Tim, Thank you for loving me and for always holding me up! I miss you every day and will love you always!

Cover photo: Naples, Italy © Tim Veney, 2016

Introduction

Mom was very aware after her 2006 diagnosis that she had dementia, and as her condition worsened she used to always say "I don't know what I'm doing!" in the most exasperated voice you can imagine. It always hurt me to my core when she'd say that and it spurred me to continue doing whatever I can to help find a cure for this dreaded disease. As mom's condition worsened I needed inspiration on many days!

Over the years, I've been inspired by many of the photos Tim and I have taken on our travels and I began writing inspirational quotes to accompany some of my favorite photos and saved them to look at when I was having a bad day. The photos really perked mom up too, and she'd say "wow" upon seeing many of the scenic views. She was amazed that Tim and I had traveled to so many places and taken all the photos ourselves. Because we loved the photos so much, I decided to publish them in a book in the hopes that they might be uplifting for others. In honor of my mom, there's no rhyme or reason or specific order to the photos, just as there's no order in mom's brain because of her dementia.

No matter who you are caring for or what disease they have, I hope our photos and quotes in this book help to refresh your spirit!

You can conquer any
situation when you
have great support!

Grand Canyon, Arizona © Tim Veney, 2016

Red Rock Canyon, Nevada © Loretta Woodward Veney, 2016

Mt. Rigi, Switzerland © Tim Veney, 2016

Copenhagen, Denmark © Tim Veney, 2016

Jungfrau, Switzerland © Tim Veney, 2016

Wherever you are, take a minute to enjoy the view!

Mt. Rigi, Switzerland © Tim Veney, 2016

Tuscany, Italy © Loretta Woodward Veney, 2016

Grand Canal Venice, Italy © Loretta Woodward Veney, 2016

Santorini, Greece © Loretta Woodward Veney, 2016

Porto Santo Stefano, Italy © Tim Veney, 2016

Cancun, Mexico © Loretta Woodward Veney, 2016

Mt Rainier, Washington © Loretta Woodward Veney, 2016

Ephesus, Turkey © Loretta Woodward Veney, 2016

Tuscany, Italy © Loretta Woodward Veney, 2016

Lucerne, Switzerland © Loretta Woodward Veney, 2016

Glacier Bay, Alaska © Tim Veney, 2016

Tuscany, Italy © Loretta Woodward Veney, 2016

Lucerne, Switzerland © Tim Veney, 2016

Glacier Bay, Alaska © Loretta Woodward Veney, 2016

Abu Simbel, Egypt © Loretta Woodward Veney, 2016

Santorini, Greece © Tim Veney, 2016

Chichen Itza, Mexico © Tim Veney, 2016

Scottsdale, Arizona © Loretta Woodward Veney, 2016

Barbados, Lesser Antilles © Tim Veney, 2016

Glacier Bay, Alaska © Tim Veney, 2016

Aswan, Egypt on the River Nile © Loretta Woodward Veney, 2016

Luxor, Egypt © Loretta Woodward Veney, 2016

Copenhagen, Denmark © Tim Veney, 2016

Tulum, Mexico, © Loretta Woodward Veney, 2016

Corfu, Greece © Tim Veney, 2016

Milan, Italy © Loretta Woodward Veney, 2016

Patience and preparation make
it easier to reach the pinnacle!

Grand Canyon West Rim © Tim Veney, 2016

St. Thomas, Virgin Islands © Loretta Woodward Veney, 2016

May your life reflect everything positive about you!

Maple Valley, WA © Loretta Woodward Veney, 2016

Mt. Rainier, WA © Loretta Woodward Veney, 2016

Rhodes, Greece © Tim Veney, 2016

Maui, Hawaii © Loretta Woodward Veney, 2016

Mt. Rainier, WA © Tim Veney, 2016

Cancun, Mexico © Loretta Woodward Veney, 2016

Shafer Trail in Moab, Utah © Loretta Woodward Veney, 2016

Porto Santo Stefano, Italy © Loretta Woodward Veney, 2016

Taking great care of everything you love can have amazing results!

Siena, Italy © Tim Veney, 2016

Slow down so life's frenetic pace
doesn't overtake you like rushing water!

Snoqualmie Falls, WA © Loretta Woodward Veney, 2016

Madrid, Spain © Tim Veney, 2016

Maui, Hawaii © Loretta Woodward Veney, 2016

Antelope Canyon, Arizona © Tim Veney, 2016

Skagway, Alaska © Loreta Woodward Veney, 2016

Zurich, Switzerland © Tim Veney, 2016

Samana, Dominican Republic © Loretta Veney, 2016

Dubai, United Arab Emirates © Tim Veney, 2016

Copenhagen, Denmark © Tim Veney, 2016

The higher you have to climb, the stronger you get!

Eze, France © Tim Veney, 2016

Junfrau, Switzerland © Tim Veney, 2016

Grand Canyon, Arizona © Tim Veney 2016

Sometimes we forget that we aren't alone in this world!

Chicago, Illinois © Tim Veney, 2016

Grand canal, Venice, Italy © Loretta Woodward Veney, 2016

Kodachrome Basin, Utah © Loretta Woodward Veney, 2016

Vancouver, Canada © Loretta Woodward Veney, 2016

From a lofty perch, you can behold the world!

Lucerne, Switzerland © Loretta Woodward Veney, 2016

Coronado, CA © Loretta Woodward Veney, 2016

Even the rain
can be tranquil!

Maui, Hawaii © Tim Veney, 2016

Martha's Vineyard © Loretta Veney Woodward, 2016

Yosemite, CA © Tim Veney, 2016

Mykonos, Greece © Tim Veney, 2016

Examine your current situation
from different vantage points!

Chicago, Illinois © Tim Veney, 2016

With the right resources your challenges sail away!

Porto Santo Stefano, Italy © Tim Veney, 2016

Martha's Vineyard © Loretta Woodward Veney, 2016

Xcaret, Mexico © Loretta Woodward Veney, 2016

Grand Canyon West Rim, Arizona © Tim Veney, 2016

Niagara Falls, Canada © Tim Veney, 2016

Luxor, Egypt © Tim Veney, 2016

Keep looking until you see the big picture!

Copenhagen, Denmark © Loretta Woodward Veney, 2016

Storms may be scary but they always pass!

Moab, Utah © Tim Veney, 2016

Paris, France © Loretta Woodward Veney, 2016

Cairo, Egypt © Loretta Woodward Veney, 2016

Life is short, so enjoy a piece of cake or pie!

Pastry shop, Lucca, Italy © Tim Veney, 2016

Sunrise at Abu Simbel, Egypt © Tim Veney, 2016

Life is tougher without the right pillars in your life!

Athens, Greece © Tim Veney, 2016

Herkimer, NY © Loretta Woodward Veney, 2016

Eze, France © Loretta Woodward Veney, 2016

Get out of the house, you may discover hidden gems!

Nice, France © Loretta Woodward Veney, 2016

Glacier Bay, Alaska © Loretta Woodward Veney, 2016

St. Croix, U.S. Virgin Islands, © Loretta Woodward Veney, 2016

You're in charge of your own palace,
don't let others overrule you!

Monaco, France © Tim Veney, 2016

Mendenhall Glacier, Alaska © Loretta Woodward Veney, 2016

Encourage the negative people in your life to fly away!

Dubai, United Arab Emirates, © Loretta Woodward Veney, 2016

Bryce Canyon, Utah © Loretta Woodward Veney, 2016

Niagara Falls, Canada © Tim Veney, 2016

Lower Antelope Canyon, AZ © Tim Veney, 2016

Natural Bridge, VA © Loretta Woodward Veney, 2016

Skyline Drive, VA © Loretta Woodward Veney, 2016

La Jolla, California © Tim Veney, 2016

Prague, Czech Republic © Loretta Woodward Veney, 2016

Road to Bryce Canyon, Utah © Loretta Woodward Veney, 2016

It's ok to lean a little when you
don't feel like standing up straight!

Pisa, Italy © Loretta Woodward Veney, 2016

Caring for yourself first ensures continued growth!

Butchart Gardens, Victoria British Columbia, © Tim Veney, 2016

Seattle, Washington, © Tim Veney, 2016

Shrine Mont, Orkney Springs, VA © Loretta Woodward Veney, 2016

Be a pillar of hope in your community!

Toledo, Spain © Loretta Woodward Veney, 2016

When someone is down, lift them up!

Salzburg, Austria, © Tim Veney, 2016

Your spirit can soar when you take a retreat!

Jungfrau, Switzerland, Tim Veney, 2016

Not even a
huge barrier
should crush
your spirit.

Arches National Park, Utah © Tim Veney, 2016

Strive to make the right moves every day!

Cancun, Mexico © Loretta Woodward Veney, 2016

Mt. Rainier National Park, © Loretta Woodward Veney, 2016

Opening
closed doors
may reveal
the answers
you need!

Madrid, Spain © Tim Veney, 2016

Make your home your sanctuary!

Maple Valley, Washington, © Tim Veney, 2016

La Jolla, CA © Loretta Woodward Veney, 2016

Clevedale Historic Inn and Gardens, Spartanburg, SC, © Loretta Woodward Veney, 2016

Vancouver, Canada © Loretta Woodward Veney, 2016

Butchart Gardens, Victoria British Columbia, © Tim Veney, 2016

What makes you magnificent is
the fact that you're different!

Hot air balloon ride, Dubai, United Arab Emirates, © Tim Veney, 2016

San Juan, Puerto Rico, © Loretta Woodward Veney, 2016

Life is short don't let that ship sail without you!

St. Thomas, US Virgin Islands, © Loretta Woodward Veney, 2016

Find an energizing outlet so stress doesn't box you in!

Aswan, Egypt © Tim Veney, 2016

Arches National Park, Utah, © Loretta Woodward Veney, 2016

Trevi Fountain, Rome, Italy, © Tim Veney, 2016

Valley of the Kings, Luxor Egypt, © Tim Veney, 2016

Road to Hana, Maui, Hawaii, © Tim Veney, 2016

Scottsdale, AZ, © Loretta Woodward Veney, 2016

Kom Ombo, Egypt, © Tim Veney

Mt. Rainier, Washington, © Tim Veney, 2016

St. Thomas, US Virgin Islands © Tim Veney, 2016

Burj Khalifa in Dubai, United Arab Emirates, © Tim Veney, 2016

The three greatest pillars of support
are your family, friends and faith!

Pyramids in Cairo, Egypt © Tim Veney, 2016

Herkimer, NY © Loretta Woodward Veney, 2016

Yosemite National Park, © Loretta Woodward Veney, 2016

When all else fails, gelato may be the answer!

Gelato shop Siena, Italy © Loretta Woodward Veney, 2016

On the toughest days, even a small accomplishment can be a triumph!

Arc de Triomphe, Paris © Loretta Woodward Veney, 2016

Shenandoah National Park, VA © Tim Veney, 2016

Maui Luau, © Tim Veney, 2016

Clinton, MD © Loretta Woodward Veney, 2016

Herkimer NY, © Loretta Woodward Veney, 2016

Self-care includes enjoying new explorations!

Maui, Hawaii, © Tim Veney, 2016

We all need an angel in our lives!

National Harbor's ICE, Washington DC, © Tim Veney, 2016

The Vatican, Rome, Italy © Loretta Woodward Veney, 2016

Antelope Canyon, Arizona © Tim Veney, 2016

Porto Santo Stefano, Italy © Tim Veney, 2016

Nice, France © Loretta Woodward Veney, 2019

Jordan Pond, Bar Harbor, Maine © Loretta Woodward Veney, 2019

Scottsdale, Arizona © Loretta Woodward Veney, 2019

Bar Harbor, Maine © Loretta Woodward Veney, 2019

Clevedale Historic Inn and Gardens, Spartanburg, South Carolina © Tim Veney, 2016

Bar Harbor, Maine © Loretta Woodward Veney, 2019

Lancaster, Pennsylvania © Loretta Woodward Veney, 2019

Brooklin, Maine © Loretta Woodward Veney, 2019

Snow Island, Maine © Loretta Woodward Veney, 2019

Owego, New York © Loretta Woodward Veney, 2019

Aswan, Egypt © Tim Veney 2016

Corfu, Greece © Tim Veney 2016

You never know where you'll find an amazing waterfall!

Greenville, South Carolina © Loretta Woodward Veney, 2019

Work Hard
Play Hard
Care Hard
Loretta Woodward Veney

Epilogue

As I look back on all the travel and camping adventures Tim and I experienced in our almost 31 years of marriage, I'm so grateful for both the memories we made and the amazing photos we took to preserve them.

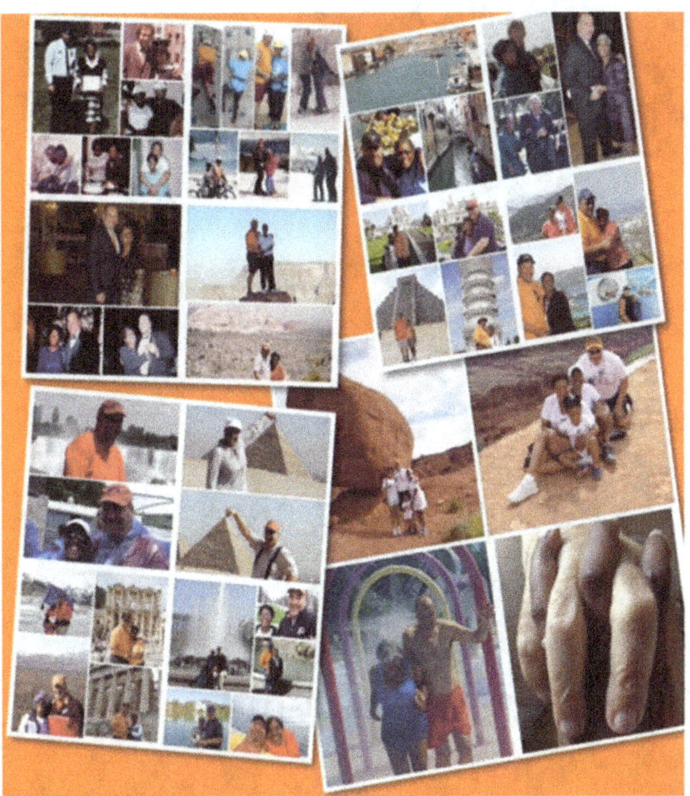

<u>Contact Information</u>

Want to book Loretta for a speaking engagement?
Loretta Woodward Veney
www.lorettaveney.com
lwveney@lorettaveney.com

Throughout her life, Loretta Woodward Veney, author of *Being My Mom's Mom* and *Colors Flowing from My Mind* has chronicled family events through journals, photos, and videos, seeking to capture every moment. After receiving the devastating news in 2006 that her beloved mother Doris was the first female in the family to suffer from dementia, Loretta began documenting the details of doctor visits, and recording people, places, and things as a substitute for her Mom's lost memory.

Loretta is a motivational speaker and trainer who has delivered more than 300 speeches and presentations on dementia and caregiving since 2014 and she offers a wealth of information and encouragement for her audiences. Loretta and her Mom been featured in articles in the Washington Post, the NY Times and AARP and appeared in a PBS special featuring Alzheimer's Caregivers.